Discover Taiwan Culture, Sports, History, Cuisine, Landmarks, People, Traditions, and many more for Kids

LOCATION

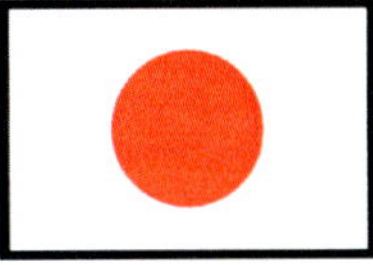

North - Faces South Korea and Japan across the East China Sea

West -
Across the Taiwan Strait from China

East-
Bounded by the Pacific Ocean

South - Near the Philippines and the South China Sea

POPULATION

23.5 million

China population
1425 Million

India Population
1428 Million

CAPITAL

Taipei

- Taipei 101, once the world's tallest building.
- The National Palace Museum, holding vast collections of Chinese imperial art.
- Taipei Zoo, home to pandas and many other animals.
- Maokong Gondola, offering scenic views.
- The creative and colorful Shilin Night Market.

CURRENCY

New Taiwan Dollar (NTD or TWD)

Denominations notes

100, 200, 500, 1000, 2000 NTD

Coins : 1, 5, 10, 20, 50 NTD

CLIMATE

A subtropical climate

Wet season

May to September

Dry season

October to April

EDUCATION

Taiwan has a 9-year compulsory education system, including elementary and junior high school. High school and university education is highly valued and competitive

LANGUAGE

Official Language

MANDARIN CHINESE

NATIONAL FLAG

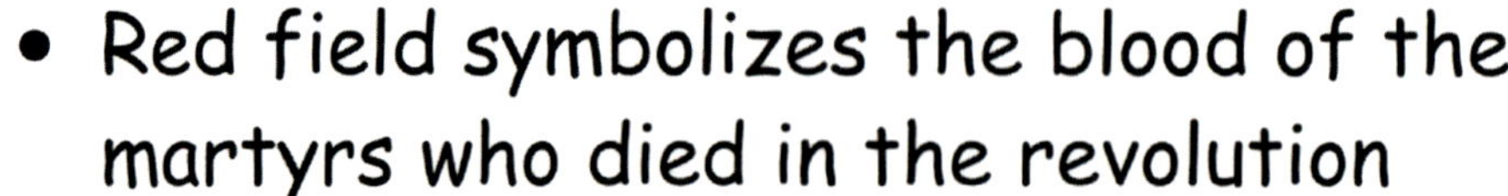

- Red field symbolizes the blood of the martyrs who died in the revolution

- White sun with twelve rays symbolizes progress and the twelve months

- Blue square represents liberty and democracy

NATIONAL ANIMAL

Formosan Black Bear

- Unique to Taiwan and known for the V-shaped white mark on its chest.
- It lives in the mountainous forests of Taiwan.
- They are omnivores and can climb trees.
- It considered a symbol of bravery and strength in Taiwanese culture.
- They are currently listed as vulnerable due to habitat loss.

NATIONAL BIRD

Taiwan Blue Magpie

- It known for its vivid blue feathers and long tail.
- Social birds that live in groups.
- It feeds on insects, small reptiles, and seeds.

- Native to Taiwan, found mostly in the mountains.
- The bird is seen as a symbol of good luck and happiness.

NATIONAL FLOWER

Plum Blossom

- It represents resilience and perseverance, as it blooms in cold winter.
- It has five petals symbolizing the five branches of the Republic of China government.
- Its fragrance and beauty are celebrated in Taiwanese culture.

- It Seen as a symbol of renewal and hope.
- Plum blossoms are white, symbolizing purity.

NATIONAL TREE

Taiwan Red Cypress

- It can live for thousands of years.
- It known for its fragrant wood, which is resistant to decay.
- It found in the mountainous areas of Taiwan

- Its wood is used for building and crafting.
- The tree symbolizes endurance and strength

TRADITIONAL MEDICINE

1) Ginseng

- Ginseng is renowned for its ability to boost energy, enhance cognitive function, and reduce stress.

2) Astragalus

- Astragalus is used to strengthen the immune system, protect the liver, and promote heart health.

3) Goji Berries

- Goji berries are touted for their high nutrient content, including antioxidants.

4) Reishi Mushroom

- Often called the "mushroom of immortality," Reishi is used to boost the immune system, reduce stress, improve sleep, and lessen fatigue.

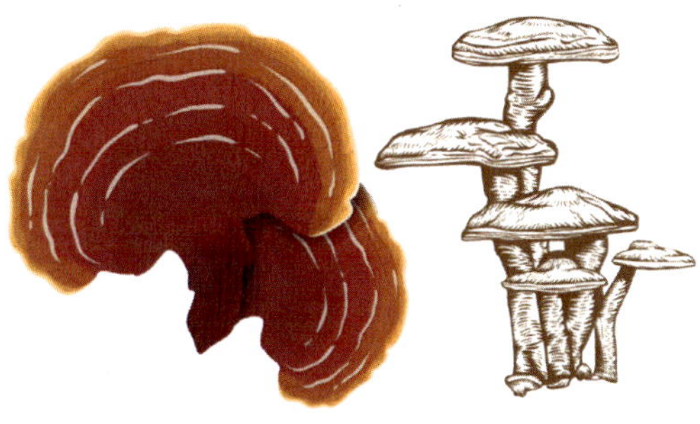

TATUN VOLCANO GROUP

- The Volcanic Playground Near a Big City.
- The Tatun Volcano Group is located very close to Taipei, the capital city of Taiwan.
- This means you can see these volcanoes from some places in the city! Imagine living near a group of volcanoes!

- A Hiker's Paradise
- The Tatun Volcano Group offers some of the best hiking trails around Taipei.
- These trails vary from easy walks that younger kids can enjoy to more challenging hikes for older adventurers.
- The trails provide beautiful views of Taipei and the surrounding natural beauty.

MAJOR NATIONAL PARKS

There are 9 National Parks in Taiwan

LAND MARKS

Chiang Kai-shek Memorial Hall

Taipei 101

Sun Moon Lake

National Palace Museum

Fort Zeelandia

Fo Guang Shan Buddha Museum

LAND MARKS

Alishan National Scenic Area

Lungshan Temple

Dragon and Tiger Pagodas

The Eternal Spring Shrine

Yushan (Jade Mountain)

Tamsui Old Street

ECONOMY

Based on

Manufacturing

Electronics

Information technology

EXPORTS

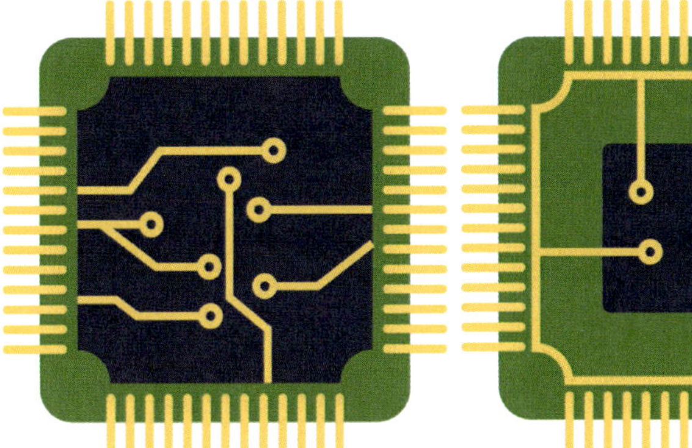

Semiconductors

Electronics

Plastics

WILD LIFE

Eco system most diverse in the world

Formosan black bear

Clouded leopard

Formosan macaque

MARINE LIFE

Eco system most diverse in the world

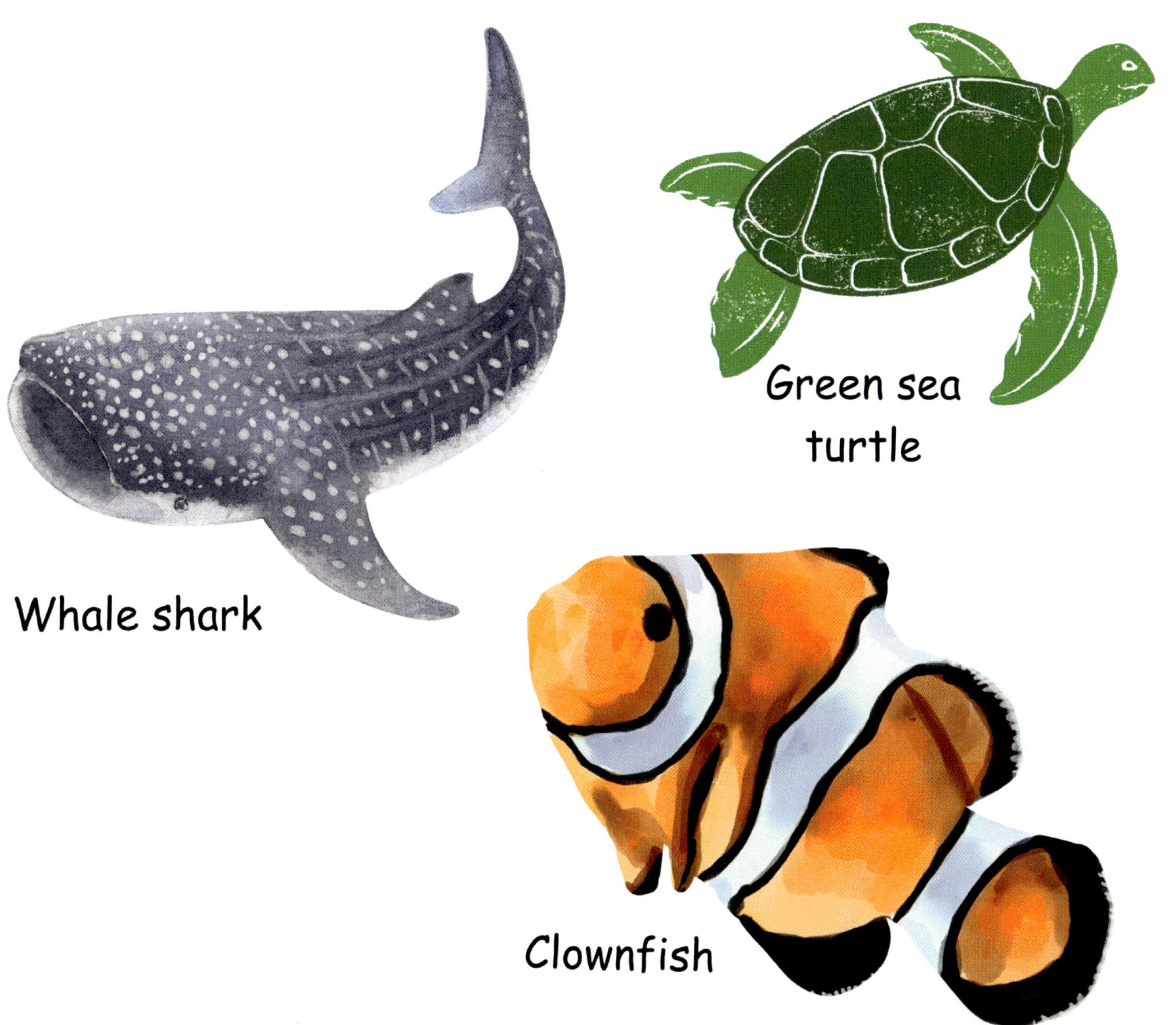

BIRDS & BUTTERFLY
Paradise for birds watchers
705 Species
400
Butterfly
varierty

SPORTS& ADVENTURES

Popular Sports are as follows

FAMOUS PEOPLE

ARTS & CRAFTS

Pottery and Ceramics

Lacquerware

Glass Art

Atayal Weaving

Bamboo Crafting

Wood Carving

Paper Cutting

CUISINE

Country has multi cultural society

Bubble Tea

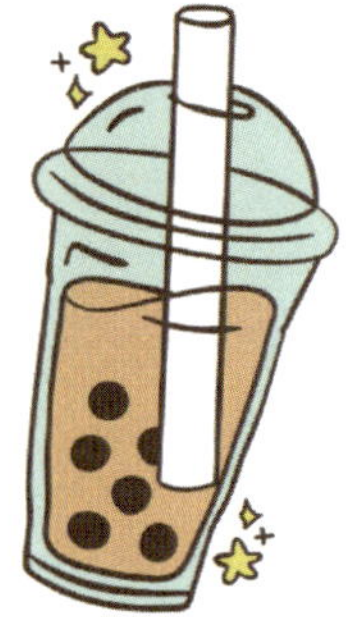

Stinky Tofu

Gua Bao

Lu Rou Fan

Beef Noodle Soup

Pineapple Cake

Fried chicken fillets

Dumplings

Oyster Omelet

Grilled squid

sashimi

Tea

UNESCO- WORLD HERITAGE SITES

Alishan Forest Railway

Tainan Historical Quarters

Penghu Archipelago

Yushan National Park

Taroko National Park

Siraya National Scenic Area

Kinmen Battlefield culture

The Tao mountain

Fort San Domingo

FESTIVALS

Dragon Boat Festival
Lantern Festival
Mid-Autumn Festival

MUSIC INSTRUMENTS

INTERNATIONAL RELATIONS

- Taiwan is known for its vibrant democracy and economic strength but faces complex international relations, especially with China.
- It has unofficial relations with many countries and is a member of some international organizations under the name "Chinese Taipei."

FUN FACTS

- Bubble Tea Wonderland
- Taiwan is the birthplace of bubble tea, a sweet drink with tapioca pearls, invented in the 1980s.

- The Skyscraper Marvel
- Taipei 101 was once the world's tallest building until 2010 and has one of the fastest elevators in the world.

- Night Market Galore
- There are over 100 night markets in Taiwan, offering delicious foods, games, and shopping.

- The Hello Kitty Heaven
- There's a Hello Kitty-themed hospital in Taiwan where everything from the decor to the uniforms features the popular character.

- The Convenience Store Capital.
- Taiwan has the highest density of convenience stores in the world. You're never too far from a 7-Eleven!

- The Garbage Truck Music
- In Taiwan, garbage trucks play music (like ice cream trucks in other countries) to notify people it's time to bring out the trash.

- The Giant Panda Diplomacy.
- Though not native to Taiwan, the Taipei Zoo is home to giant pandas as a symbol of friendship with China.

- The Island of Temples.
- There are more than 15,000 temples across Taiwan, showcasing the island's rich religious culture.

- The Plastic-Free Pioneer

- Taiwan is a leader in environmental protection, planning to ban single-use plastics completely by 2030.

- The Milkfish Mania

- Milkfish is a popular food in Taiwan, and there's even a museum dedicated to it.

- The Ghost Festival

- One of Taiwan's unique festivals is the Ghost Festival, where it's believed the spirits of the dead roam the earth.

- The Anping Tree House

- A former warehouse taken over by a banyan tree, creating a natural architectural wonder.

- Hot Spring Heaven

- Taiwan has one of the highest concentrations and varieties of hot springs in the world.

- The Sun Moon Lake.

- Taiwan's largest lake is named for its parts that resemble the sun and the moon.

- A Language Treasure Trove.

- Besides Mandarin, various indigenous languages and dialects are spoken in Taiwan, showcasing its cultural diversity.

- The Pingxi Sky Lantern Festival

- Visitors can write wishes on sky lanterns and release them into the night sky, creating a magical sight.

Made in the USA
Las Vegas, NV
03 March 2025